www.thegreatchiweenie.com

ISBN-13 978-0-9814900-1-4
ISBN-10 0-9814900-1-8

All Photographs by:
Cubby Cashen and
Megan Cordes.

WARNING: Riding a bicycle can be dangerous. Please wear all
safety equipment and follow all the laws and regulations when riding
a bicycle. Gu is safely harnessed into the backpack in which
he rides, but is still at risk of injury due to any accidents or falls.
Wear a helmet. PLEASE RIDE SAFE.

Teachers, Principals, and Businesses, for bulk purchasing or promotionals,
please contact Cubby at thegreatchiweenie@hotmail.com.

The Great Chiweenie presents

Around the Hood

by GU
and
Cubby Cashen

The Great Chiweenie Productions
P.O. Box 669
Cambria, CA 93428
thegreatchiweenie@hotmail.com
www.thegreatchiweenie.com

Note from the Author:

Hey! My Name is Gu, a.k.a. "The Great Chiweenie" (Act like the I is silent CH-Weenie). I am part-dachshund and part-chihuahua and I travel with my adopted parents, Megan and Cub. With the help of my family and friends I put together a little poem from my eyes about a mountain bike trip around Mount Hood in Northern Oregon. I hope you enjoy.

Megan, Cub and I,
took off on a trip.
From what we'd heard,
the Northwest is so hip.

Around the Hood,
pavement, rocks, and sand,
With views of the Mountain,
that were oh so grand.

Cub was the silly one,
riding only one gear,
but it didn't take long,
till he wished the end near.

Megan, on the other hand,
rode whichever gear she liked.
She waited for the Cubster
and she smiled while she biked.

I rode with Cub
on days one and three.
While days two and four,
with Megan I would be.

In the backpack,
I spent most of the day,
but during the night,
the huts we would stay.

As we woke in the mornings,
I'd come out of my den,
and the day of long riding,
was soon to begin.

As day 1 began,
we climbed up many hills,
with glances of Mt. Hood,
with downhills and thrills.

7

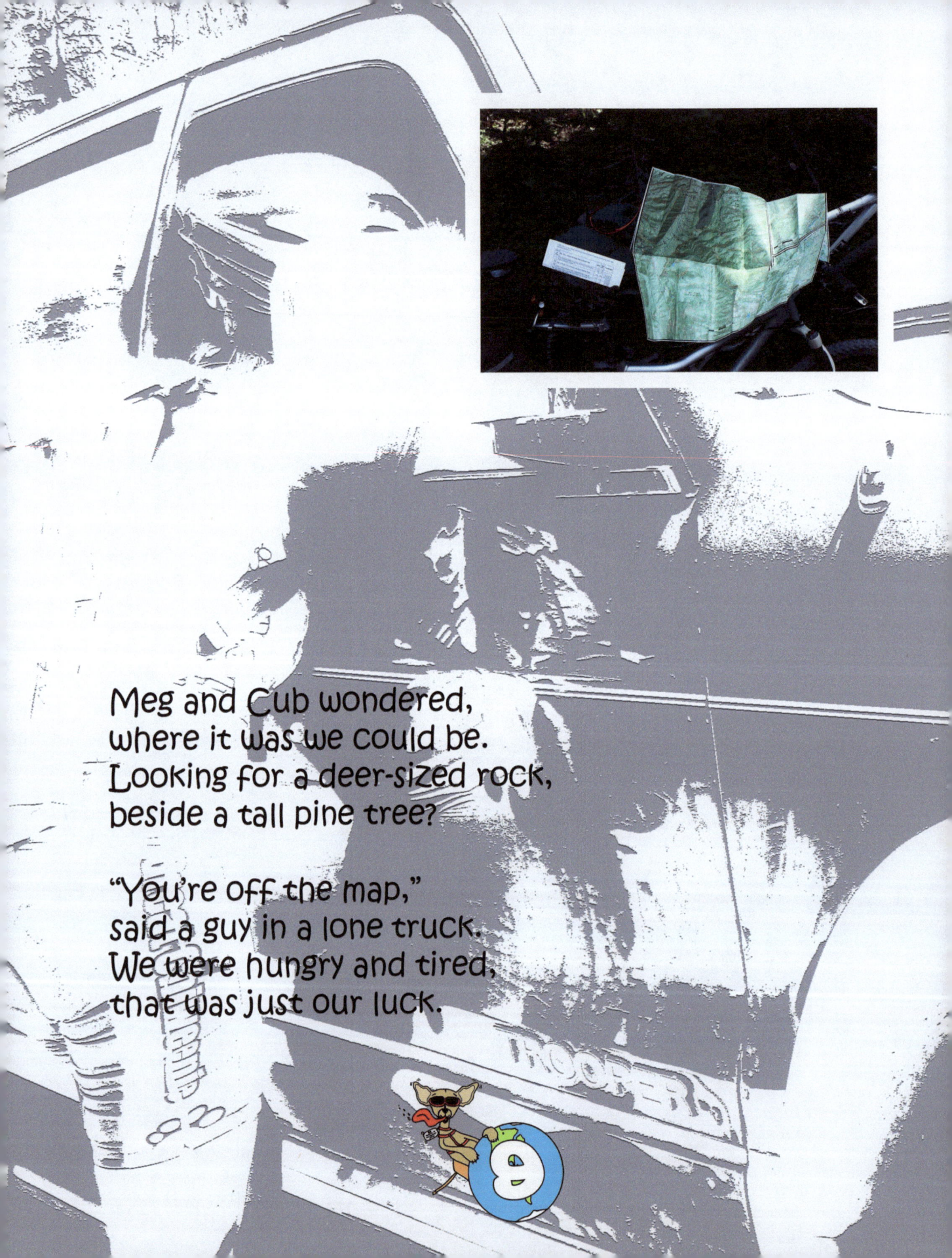

Meg and Cub wondered,
where it was we could be.
Looking for a deer-sized rock,
beside a tall pine tree?

"You're off the map,"
said a guy in a lone truck.
We were hungry and tired,
that was just our luck.

Luckily the phone
worked in just that place.
We talked to the owners,
now on the map we could trace.

We cruised to the hut,
eating as much as we could.
Looking through the cupboard,
was the only moment we stood.

Climbing most of the morning,
day 2 we would start.
when we walked through the snow,
we started to lose heart.

But downhills were to come,
and boy were they fast.
I knew I truly wanted
them to forever last.

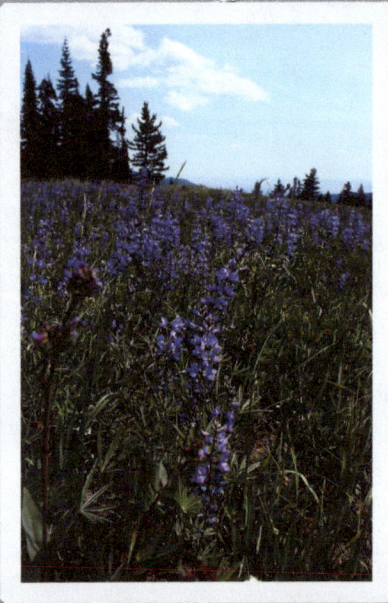

Smells went up my nose.
Winds pressed against my face.
My ears flopped up and back,
as if we were in a race.

Next to a river bed
the ground was mostly flat.
Children playing on downed logs,
while the others just sat.

Looking over at us,
"Did you see the dog on their back?"
Parents would laugh,
and we would continue on track.

Cub's legs were toast
but we were soon to be done.
The night would fly by.
Day 3 had begun.

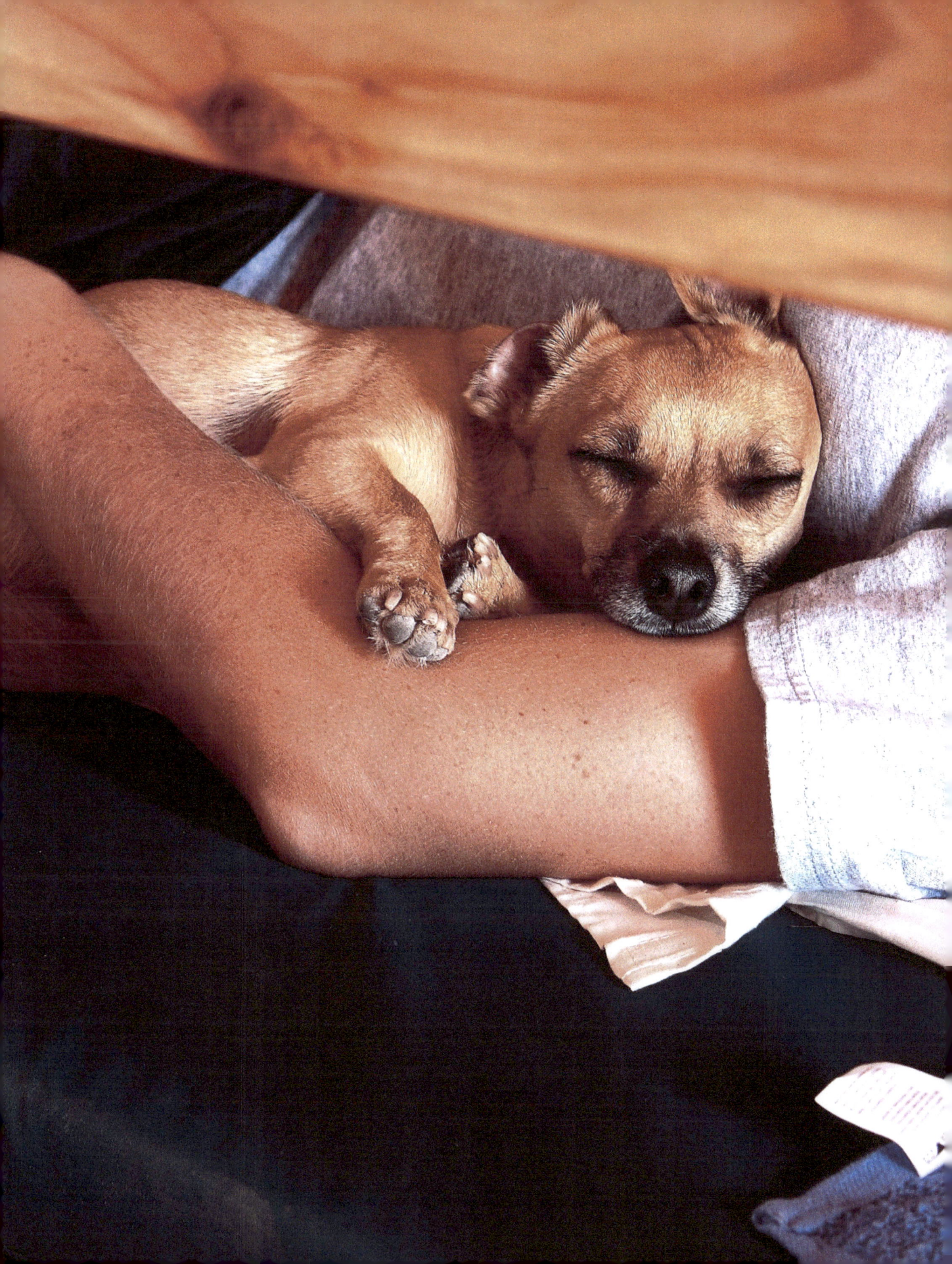

We started with a small climb,
and passed the PCT.
While Cub and Megan ate
I went wee on a tree.

A long downhill followed
as we passed many bikers.
Finally slowing near houses,
as we came upon many hikers.

BARLOW ROAD

FIRST ROAD BUILT OVER CASCADE RANGE
IN 1845-1846 BY
SAMUEL K. BARLOW (1792-1867)
AN OREGON PIONEER FROM KENTUCKY

WAMIC	MILES	32
DALLES CALIFORNIA HIGHWAY	"	38
MAUPIN	"	48

A busy road,
before we turned off that street.
A quiet paved road,
man that was a treat.

Names painted on the road,
as if we were in France.
Armstrong, Merckx, Pantani,
Cub would read in a trance.

The views were amazing
as we neared the top.
Cub, Megan and I
would enjoy our last stop.

Drip, drip, drop,
as it sounded like rain.
Fog had approached,
which seemed to ease the pain.

28

Mt. Hood was gone,
overtaken by the fog.
Our last day we began
in a little bit of a sog.

Quiet roads early,
but the roads soon were packed.
We pedaled onward,
motivation we did not lack.

Through Hood River,
and then up the hill.
Back to the car,
that looked very still.

We packed up the car
and went to my favorite place.
We always end a great trip
with ice cream on my face.

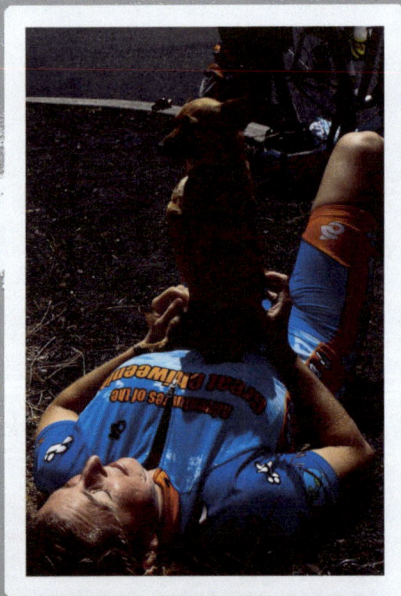

Keep up to date on all of our new adventures at **www.thegreatchiweenie.com.** Check back often.

Adopt a pet. Ride a bike. Smile.